BACK TO THE BEACH

Written and Illustrated by Mo MacPhail

Copyright © 2017 Mo MacPhail.

All rights reserved. No part of this book may be used or reproduced by any means, graphic, electronic, or mechanical, including photocopying, recording, taping or by any information storage retrieval system without the written permission of the author except in the case of brief quotations embodied in critical articles and reviews.

Balboa Press books may be ordered through booksellers or by contacting:

Balboa Press
A Division of Hay House
1663 Liberty Drive
Bloomington, IN 47403
www.balboapress.com
1 (877) 407-4847

Because of the dynamic nature of the Internet, any web addresses or links contained in this book may have changed since publication and may no longer be valid. The views expressed in this work are solely those of the author and do not necessarily reflect the views of the publisher, and the publisher hereby disclaims any responsibility for them.

Any people depicted in stock imagery provided by Thinkstock are models, and such images are being used for illustrative purposes only. Certain stock imagery © Thinkstock.

ISBN: 978-1-5043-7602-0 (sc)
ISBN: 978-1-5043-7603-7 (e)

Library of Congress Control Number: 2017903226

Print information available on the last page.

Balboa Press rev. date: 03/17/2017

There's a particular saying out there that states, you can never go back. However in my heart I know this is not true. For there is a place we can always go back to. It is a magical, mystical place we are invited to return again and again in order to move forward. It is the place where repeated visits bring us back to the knowing and the essence of why we are here. In our family we have many of these back to places, but our favorite "Back To" place is the beach at Sandy Neck, in Cape Cod, Massachusetts, where the smell of its salt water calls a soul back to life. This book chronicles memories from our beach as they propel us forward to live lives with purpose and promise. My hope is that upon reading this book, a "Back To" journey will begin for you.

Back to the beach

Back in our truck

Launching our boat

To find clams we will shuck.

Back in the water,

Back on the rocks,

Paddling a kayak,

To the shore we will flock.

Back to the house

With Adirondack chairs,

Eating our ice cream

Without a care.

Back to the stars,

It's extra bright at the beach,

An astronomy lesson,

Douglas will teach.

Back to the Sweet Shop

For soda pop candy,

Exploring our world

Finding treasures quite sandy.

Outside the house,

We go back to the shower

To wash and to clean,

While smelling the flowers.

Back to the lighthouse,

It stands proud and tall,

Guarding the tide

As it rises and falls.

Back to the bridge,

In the old town,

If you jump off the side,

There's no diving down.

Back to the Dunes,

Sandy mountains beg climbing,

Pretending there's pirates,

Whose treasures are hiding.

Back to the dock

Where whale watching starts,

Soon one will view

An ocean's beating heart.

Back to summer's embracing reach,

Back to,

Back to,

Back to the beach!

CPSIA information can be obtained
at www.ICGtesting.com
Printed in the USA
BVOW05s2146310317
480031BV00002B/3/P